WOMEN IN STEM

WOMEN IN
EARTH AND SPACE
EXPLORATION

by Tammy Gagne

Content Consultant
Linda M. French, PhD
Professor of Physics
Illinois Wesleyan University

Core Library

An Imprint of Abdo Publishing
abdopublishing.com

abdopublishing.com

Published by Abdo Publishing, a division of ABDO, PO Box 398166, Minneapolis, Minnesota 55439. Copyright © 2017 by Abdo Consulting Group, Inc. International copyrights reserved in all countries. No part of this book may be reproduced in any form without written permission from the publisher. Core Library™ is a trademark and logo of Abdo Publishing.

Printed in the United States of America, North Mankato, Minnesota
032016
092016

Cover Photo: NASA
Interior Photos: NASA, 1, 12, 15, 25, 26, 34, 45; iStockphoto, 4, 7, 43; RIA Novosti/Science Source, 10; Peter Burnett/iStockphoto, 18; John Irwin Collection/AIP/Science Source, 21; SPL/Science Source, 23; Robbie Shone/Science Source, 28; Shutterstock Images, 31; Al Grillo/AP Images, 38; Claus Lunau/Science Source, 39

Editor: Arnold Ringstad
Series Designer: Laura Polzin

Cataloging-in-Publication Data
Names: Gagne, Tammy, author.
Title: Women in Earth and space exploration / by Tammy Gagne.
Description: Minneapolis, MN : Abdo Publishing, [2017] | Series: Women in
     STEM | Includes bibliographical references and index.
Identifiers: LCCN 2015960511 | ISBN 9781680782660 (lib. bdg.) |
     ISBN 9781680776775 (ebook)
Subjects: LCSH: Earth (Planet)--Juvenile literature. | Outer planets--Juvenile
     literature. | Planets--Juvenile literature. | Outer space--Exploration--Juvenile
     literature. | Solar system--Juvenile literature. | Astronomers--Juvenile
     literature.
Classification: DDC 523--dc23
LC record available at http://lccn.loc.gov/2015960511

CONTENTS

EXPLORING OUR WORLD AND BEYOND

What do you picture when you hear the word *explorer*? You may think of adventurous men who lived hundreds of years ago and sailed their ships across the seas. Or you might picture the astronauts who walked on the moon in 1969. Most of history's famous explorers were men. But women have made pioneering explorations too. Many of today's explorers are women. These scientists and

Women explore and study the remote regions of our planet.

Careers in Exploration

Explorers are making exciting discoveries in many fields. Here are just a few of them:

- Geologists study Earth's natural processes. Their work helps predict disasters such as earthquakes and landslides. This can save lives.

- Deep-sea biologists study life far beneath the ocean's surface.

- Marine geologists study the ocean floor. They try to predict where volcanoes will emerge.

- Planetary astronomers study other planets.

- Solar astronomers study Earth's sun. Stellar astronomers study other stars.

adventurers make amazing discoveries. Some explore Earth's surface. Others dive deep into the oceans. And some blast into space on powerful rockets.

Giant Leaps for Womankind

Today more women than ever are entering science, technology, engineering, and math (STEM) fields. These fields include physical science and Earth science. These two areas of study are central to exploring our world. More than half of the women who earned STEM college degrees in 2009 majored

Studying hard in science classes helps prepare young women for careers in exploration.

in physical and Earth sciences. They studied subjects such as astronomy, geology, and physics.

STEM graduates are finding careers in higher numbers too. Many work at the National Aeronautics and Space Administration (NASA). NASA has hired large numbers of women in recent years. In 2013 37 percent of the space agency's new employees were female. Half of its eight new astronauts that year were women.

Hohonu Moana Expedition

In 2015 the National Oceanic and Atmospheric Administration (NOAA) explored the deep waters off the Hawaiian Islands. This project was called the Hohonu Moana expedition. Kelley Elliott led the expedition. Her team explored for 12 weeks. It identified at-risk marine habitats. It located large communities of deep-sea life, such as corals and sponges. It also collected data on the region's geological history.

Imagine the excitement of working 155 miles (250 km) above Earth at the International Space Station (ISS). Astronauts there zoom around the planet at more than 17,000 miles per hour (27,400 km/h). Perhaps you would rather walk on the ocean floor in a sturdy diving suit. Incredible forms of life lurk in these dark corners of the sea. Or maybe you would prefer the thrill of studying active volcanoes. Red-hot lava flows from deep below the ground up to the surface at these sites. Pioneering women have explored all of these places. They brave extreme conditions in some of the most amazing locations on and off the planet. They are making exciting discoveries about the world around us.

FURTHER EVIDENCE

Chapter One includes information about exploration careers. What was one of the chapter's main points? What evidence was given to support that point? Check out the article at the link below. Choose a quote from the piece that relates to this chapter. Does this quote support the author's main point? Does it make a new point?

Inspiring Women in STEM

mycorelibrary.com/women-in-exploration

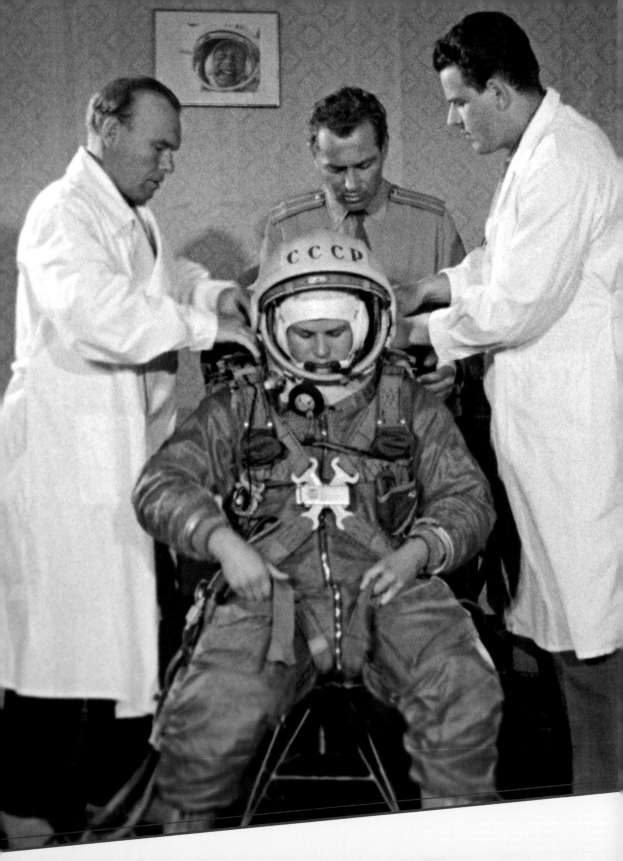

CHAPTER TWO

WOMEN IN SPACE

Women have been exploring outer space since 1963. In that year, Valentina Tereshkova became the first woman launched into orbit. A Vostok-K rocket boosted her into space from the Soviet Union. She spent nearly three days in Earth orbit. Many women have followed in her footsteps.

Tereshkova prepares for her mission.

Ride trained for five years before going into space.

Sally Ride

Astronaut Sally Ride was the first US woman in space. She flew her first mission in 1983. She traveled on the space shuttle *Challenger*. It was the seventh space shuttle mission. The five-person crew had many goals. One was to release two satellites. Satellites let people in different parts of the world communicate. A person uses a device to send a signal from the ground to the satellite. The satellite beams the signals back down to another location.

Ride controlled *Challenger*'s robotic arm. She used the arm to put the satellites into place. The arm can also be used to grab a satellite for repairs. Ride was part of the team that developed the robotic arm.

Pamela Melroy

Pamela Melroy traveled to space three times. On her third trip in 2007, she served as mission commander. She is one of the only women to command a US spacecraft.

On her first mission, Melroy worked on the

ISS. She helped create a docking station for future missions. Her second mission added systems to make spacewalks easier. Her final trip was to install a new module on the ISS. It is called Harmony. The module has room and equipment for European and Japanese laboratories.

The *Challenger* Disaster

Being an astronaut comes with risk. This was especially clear on January 28, 1986. On that day the space shuttle *Challenger* exploded shortly after liftoff. Seven people died in the disaster. One was mission specialist Judy Resnik. Another was Christa McAuliffe, who was not a professional astronaut. McAuliffe was aboard as the first teacher in space. She had planned to teach lessons to students back on the ground.

Samantha Cristoforetti

Samantha Cristoforetti was born in Italy in 1977. She studied aerospace engineering in college and focused on rocket technology. Cristoforetti then joined the Italian Air Force. She became a fighter pilot. This experience made her a natural fit to become an

Cristoforetti took many photos from the ISS.

astronaut. She joined the European Space Agency in 2009.

Cristoforetti launched on her first mission in 2014. She became Italy's first female astronaut and set the record for the longest single space mission by a woman. She lived and worked on the ISS for 199 days. While in space, Cristoforetti used Twitter to send photos and messages back to Earth. By 2015 she had more than 600,000 followers on the social networking website.

A reporter once asked Cristoforetti if she considered herself a role model for young women. She replied that she hoped to be a role model for all young people. She doesn't think being a female astronaut makes her different. Cristoforetti believes she is doing the same job as her male coworkers. She says she has equal respect for her male and female role models.

Mae Jemison was the first African-American female astronaut. In an interview, Jemison discussed how she prepared for the weightlessness of space:

> There's no such thing as antigravity training. That's one of those misconceptions that people have. Gravity is everywhere—it's just that we're weightless when we're flying on the shuttle. But gravity is all around you. . . . We do several things to train for weightlessness. Sometimes we train in a big pool of water called the "neutral buoyancy trainer." We put on our extravehicular activity suits (the big white suits), and then we remain neutrally buoyant—we don't float and we don't sink. All the astronauts who are up in space are now trained this way. There is a trainer we use that makes us truly weightless. It's a big airplane called the KC-135. It flies in parabolas—big "u" shapes—up and down. It's like a big roller coaster. At the top of the loop, you have about 20 seconds of weightlessness.

> Source: "Dr. Mae Jemison Interview." NASA: Challenging the Space Frontier. Scholastic, March 15, 2001. Web. Accessed January 29, 2016.

Consider Your Audience

Write about Jemison's training for a new audience, such as a younger brother or sister. How would you explain weightlessness training? If you need more information, ask an adult for help finding another source about how astronauts train.

CHAPTER THREE

THE WORK OF FEMALE ASTRONOMERS

Astronomers study the universe. This work involves amazing distances. The universe is so large that it takes light billions of years to cross it. These distances are much too vast for astronauts to travel. Telescopes let astronomers study faraway planets, stars, and galaxies.

Telescopes are important tools for astronomy.

Vera Rubin

Vera Rubin became interested in astronomy as a child. But joining the field was a struggle. She graduated from Vassar College with a degree in astronomy in 1948. She applied to graduate school at Princeton University, but she was rejected. Women were not allowed in the program at that time. Rubin enrolled at Cornell University instead and continued working.

Rubin studied the rotation of galaxies. Her work helped detect dark matter. This invisible substance is thought to make up much of the universe. Yet scientists know almost nothing about it. They are still

Caroline Herschel

Caroline Herschel was born in Germany in 1750. She grew up to be one of the world's first female astronomers. As a young woman, she moved to England to live with her brother, William. Caroline began helping him make telescopes. Over time she became fascinated with astronomy. In 1786 she became the first woman to discover a comet. In the next 11 years, she would discover seven more.

Rubin made important discoveries at a time when women were not widely accepted in astronomy.

studying it today. Rubin's efforts laid the groundwork for today's research into dark matter's mysteries.

Wendy Freedman

Wendy Freedman studies the expansion rate of the universe. The Canadian-American astronomer is in charge of creating the Giant Magellan Telescope

(GMT). This massive observatory in South America will stand approximately 141 feet (43 m) tall. Its builders plan to complete it in 2025.

GMT will help scientists look into distant space. The light it will see from faraway stars left those stars billions of years ago. This means that astronomers can use the telescope to literally look into the past. Freedman hopes it may even be able to show them how the universe began.

Carolyn Porco

The *Cassini* spacecraft left Earth in 1997. Seven years later, in 2004, it reached Saturn. It entered

Many Moons

Look at this image showing Saturn and a few of its 62 known moons. What kinds of things do you think astronomers could discover about these moons using telescopes? Could more information be discovered by sending a robotic spacecraft to Saturn? What about sending astronauts? Write out the pros and cons of each type of mission.

orbit around the planet. The spacecraft took pictures and sent back data. One of the scientists studying *Cassini*'s results is Carolyn Porco. She is the leader of the *Cassini* imaging science team. This group studies Saturn, the planet's moons, and its rings.

In 2006 Porco's team made an exciting announcement. The team had been studying icy geysers on Saturn's moon Enceladus. Porco reported that her team found evidence for an ocean under this moon's surface. Scientists found even stronger evidence in 2015. The way the moon wobbles shows the surface is not frozen all the way through. This suggests Enceladus has an ocean. Scientists believe that if life exists outside of Earth, it may be in the ocean of Enceladus.

New Horizons

One of the most exciting space events of 2015 took place far from Earth. In July the *New Horizons* spacecraft reached Pluto after a nine-year journey. Pluto is a dwarf planet. It is about 40 times farther from the sun than Earth is.

One-quarter of the people on the *New Horizons* team are women. This is a much higher number of women than on previous missions. These women are mission planners, scientists, and engineers. Among

Some of the women behind *New Horizons* pose in January 2006 in front of the rocket that later launched the spacecraft to Pluto.

The *New Horizons* mission took amazing photos of Pluto, bottom, and its largest moon, Charon.

them is deputy project scientist Cathy Olkin. She says the gender of her team members isn't a big issue: "*New Horizons* is about a group of talented, smart people who are passionate about the mission. That's what makes *New Horizons* awesome."

INCREDIBLE EARTH SCIENTISTS

Space is an exciting place to study. However, much of Earth remains unexplored too. Many fields involve exploring our planet's land and seas. Geologists study the planet's changing surface. Oceanographers explore the oceans. Volcanologists investigate volcanoes. They try to predict when and where they will erupt.

Geologists study the Earth's surface and everything below it.

Kayla Iacovino

Studying volcanoes has taken Kayla Iacovino places where few Americans have set foot. Out of all the active volcanoes in the world, Mount Erebus is the farthest south. It is located on the continent of Antarctica. Mount Paektu is in North Korea. This secretive country has been closed to most of the world for decades. Iacovino has studied both of these magma-filled mountains.

Mount Paektu's location makes it difficult for scientists to study. For years many scientists were

Mount Paektu has a large lake at its peak.

unaware that it existed at all. Iacovino was given special permission to enter the country and work with North Korean scientists. She learned about Mount Paektu and shared her own knowledge with her North Korean partners.

Emily Klein

Emily Klein is a marine geochemist at Duke University. Like Iacovino, her work involves volcanoes. Part of Klein's job is studying the chemical makeup of lava in the ocean. Following an eruption, this material hardens on the ocean floor. By studying the lava, she can understand what is happening at the bottom of the sea.

Her work has helped other volcanologists understand the pressure and temperatures magma goes through. Once it breaks through the surface, it is known as lava. Klein's research has helped scientists determine where the magma comes from. One of her biggest discoveries is that magma does not always flow straight up. Sometimes it travels sideways. It may rise far from where it originated.

Ashanti Johnson

Ashanti Johnson is an aquatic scientist. She

Vast Seas

Oceans cover about 70 percent of Earth. They are very important to human life. They have a major effect on the world's climate and weather. We use the oceans to get from one place to another. We use them for swimming, boating, and scuba diving. We rely on them for fish and other seafood. However, more than 95 percent of underwater areas remains unexplored. There is still much for scientists to learn about our oceans.

studies radioactive material in Earth's waterways. When ice melts, the water runs off into the surrounding soil. It can carry radioactive pollution into the ocean. Johnson has shown how pollution in Russia has traveled all the way to Alaska. Along the way, it can harm fish.

She now studies waterways off the coast of Georgia. Her research shows what might happen to dangerous pollution after a nuclear accident. She also studies the best ways to clean up after such an event.

EXPLORE ONLINE

Chapter Four includes information about the work of volcanologists. The website below focuses on the same subject. As you know, every source is different. How is the information at this site different from what you have read in the chapter? How is it the same? What can you learn from this website about the field of volcanology?

About Volcanologists

mycorelibrary.com/women-in-exploration

CHAPTER FIVE

FUTURE FEMALE EXPLORERS

any female explorers want to help girls interested in these fields. Some of these women grew up when female students were discouraged from studying science. Astronomer Wendy Freedman had a high school science teacher who discouraged female students. He would sometimes say to the class, "The girls don't have to

Mae Jemison dreamed of becoming an astronaut as a child. In 1992 she became the first African-American woman to fly into space.

listen to this." When sharing this story with others, Freedman says she chose to ignore that statement.

Sally Ride, Still Inspiring

Sally Ride died in 2012, but her legacy lives on in many ways. One of them is through the Sally Ride Science Summer Camps for Girls. Female students in fourth through ninth grade can participate in these camps. Sessions run throughout the summer. They are held at universities in California and Massachusetts.

Aspire 2 Inspire

NASA created the Aspire 2 Inspire program in 2011. Its goal is to encourage girls to study math and science. The program is run entirely by female NASA employees. It focuses on space exploration. However, it stresses that working at NASA is only one of many career paths. Young women can visit the Aspire 2 Inspire website to learn about a wide range of STEM jobs.

Another program named after the late astronaut involves a camera. It is known as the Sally Ride EarthKAM. Ride herself started this program in 1995.

When she flew into space, she was amazed by the beauty of Earth. She wanted to share this perspective with others. She asked NASA to set up a camera in space. Middle-school students can request photos of specific places on Earth. That camera is now part of the ISS. More than 600,000 kids have taken part in this program.

Erupting Interests

Researchers at the Geophysical Institute in Fairbanks, Alaska, provided learning opportunities to girls. Graduate students at the university met with girls

Scientists closely watch Redoubt Volcano for signs of a future eruption.

as young as eight to teach them about subjects such as volcanology. At the school's Volcano Monitoring Room, the grad students taught the students how to examine rocks. They also showed footage of Redoubt Volcano, which erupted in Alaska in 1989.

If You Prefer Water

Science camps also exist for girls interested in oceanography. The University of South Florida

The Underwater Landscape

Look at this drawing of the ocean floor near Japan. Notice that there are peaks and valleys even beneath the ocean's surface. What challenges do you think underwater explorers face? Why might exploring the deepest parts of the ocean be difficult? Can you think of any creative solutions to these problems?

College of Marine Science hosts one such program. This free three-week adventure takes place every summer in Saint Petersburg, Florida. It includes an entire day at sea aboard a research boat. Students also go on coastal field trips.

The instructors include graduate students and researchers. Campers have an opportunity to interview these scientists about their careers. Some former campers even go on to participate in the program as counselors. They pass on what they have learned.

Whether you want to explore the oceans, volcanoes, or other planets, there are many fields of science to pursue. Many women have already made great strides in these careers. There is plenty of new territory underground, below the waves, and in deep space just waiting to be explored.

Winston Yeung's two young daughters launched a balloon to the edge of space in 2015. The event caught the attention of NASA. Their father explained how the girls, just 8 and 10, managed this incredible task.

> I'm not one to give advice, but I would say, at least for our girls and our family, [let] them have as much hands-on opportunities as possible. I mean that sounds a little trite, but for us it's literally hands-on where we do a lot of projects in the garage, and we do a lot of stuff where we [are] making things and building things and fixing things. Yeah, they can use a power screwdriver, and sure, they can use a handsaw with the right safety conditions. We've been doing that pretty early on. Now they're at the point where they can operate some of these things on their own, safely and supervised. At least now I think they have the confidence to start to build some of these things by themselves.

Source: Todd Bishop. "Seattle Girls Launch a Balloon Spacecraft to the Edge of Space, and NASA Takes Note." GeekWire. Geek Wire, September 11, 2015. Web. Accessed January 29, 2016.

What's the Big Idea?

Take a close look at Yeung's words. What is his main idea? What evidence does he include to support this point? Come up with a few sentences that support the main idea of this passage.

Explore the Night Sky

Does your city have an observatory or planetarium? These are excellent places to learn about astronomy. They often hold presentations or classes. Ask a parent, teacher, or librarian to help you find an interesting event to attend.

There's a Book about That

Go to your local library and search for books about oceanography, volcanology, or space travel. Which parts of these fields interest you the most? Try to find books about these specific topics. What new information can you find about your chosen topics?

Write to Someone in the Field

Write a letter or e-mail to a woman who works in your favorite exploration field. Ask questions that have come to mind while learning about her career.

Take a Class

Math and science classes are important foundations for any STEM career in exploration. Talk to your math or science teachers about how their particular subject relates to exploration. How might this class help you in a future career in exploration?

Say What?

Learning about exploration can mean learning new vocabulary. Find five words in this book that you had never seen or heard before. Use a dictionary to find out what they mean. Write down the meaning of each word. Then use each word in a new sentence.

Take a Stand

NASA retired the space shuttle in 2011. By 2016 the United States did not yet have a new spacecraft to take astronauts into space. Do you think it is important for people to travel into space? Or should robots do space exploration instead? Write a paragraph explaining your opinion.

You Are There

Imagine you are a volcanologist. Where would you enjoy doing your research? Write a short paragraph about what you would want to learn about volcanoes in this location.

Why Do I Care?

What benefits can space exploration have for people on Earth? Write a paragraph about how the technologies and discoveries of space exploration can help improve people's lives.

GLOSSARY

comet
a bright heavenly body that develops a cloudy tail of dust as it moves closer to the sun in its orbit

docking
the joining of two spacecraft in orbit

filter
to make cleaner by removing unwanted matter from a liquid or gas

legacy
objects and ideas left behind when a person retires or dies

magma
hot melted rock that is found deep underground

misconception
a wrong or mistaken idea

observatory
a building that contains telescopes and other astronomy equipment

satellite
an object or vehicle intended to orbit Earth, the moon, or another body in space

LEARN MORE

Books

Aguilar, David A. *Space Encyclopedia.* Washington, DC: National Geographic, 2013.

Arnold, Eric. *Volcanoes! Mountains of Fire.* New York: Random House, 2013.

Maquitty, Miranda. *Ocean.* New York: DK, 2014.

Websites

To learn more about Women in STEM, visit **booklinks.abdopublishing.com**. These links are routinely monitored and updated to provide the most current information available.

Visit **mycorelibrary.com** for free additional tools for teachers and students.

INDEX

ABOUT THE AUTHOR

Tammy Gagne has written more than 100 books for both adults and children. She resides in northern New England with her husband and son. One of her favorite pastimes is visiting schools to talk to children about the writing process.